Maddie Perring

Gondellied

By

Felix Mendelssohn

For Solo Piano

(1837)

Wo010

GONDELLIED
für das Pianoforte
von
FELIX MENDELSSOHN BARTHOLDY.

Allegretto non troppo.

Lightning Source UK Ltd.
Milton Keynes UK
258633UK00002B/12